Contents

Schola████████████les

A READING GUIDE TO

Where the Red Fern Grows

by Wilson Rawls

Laurie Rozakis, Ph.D.

SCHOLASTIC
REFERENCE

Library of Congress Cataloging-in-Publication Data
Scholastic BookFiles: A Reading Guide to Where the Red Fern Grows by Wilson Rawls/written by Laurie Rozakis.
p. cm.
Summary: Discusses the writing, characters, plot, and themes of this 1961 novel in which a young boy living in the Ozarks trains his two redbone hounds to be champion hunters.
Includes bibliographical references (p.).
1. Rawls, Wilson. Where the Red Fern Grows—Juvenile literature.
2. Ozark Mountains—In literature—Juvenile literature.   3. Boys in literature—Juvenile literature.   4. Dogs in literature—Juvenile literature.   [1. Rawls, Wilson. Where the Red Fern Grows.
2. American literature—History and criticism.]   I. Title: A Reading Guide to Where the Red Fern Grows by Wilson Rawls.   II. Title.
PS3568.A854 W4837   2003
813'.54—dc21   2002191231
0-439-46375-0

10 9 8 7 6 5 4 3 2 1   03 04 05 06 07

Composition by Brad Walrod/High Text Graphics, Inc.
Cover and interior design by Red Herring Design

Printed in the U.S.A.   23
First printing, July 2003

"I am an ardent fly fisherman and a hunter. I wouldn't trade a good bedroll by a blue mountain stream for the best bed in the Waldorf-Astoria."

—Wilson Rawls

The Waldorf-Astoria is a big, fancy hotel in New York City. Most people would like to sleep in a fancy hotel, in a soft bed under a fluffy blanket. Wilson Rawls, however, liked sleeping under the stars in his sleeping bag much better. He loved the outdoors because he felt so at home there. Since his early childhood, Rawls was close to nature.

Woodrow Wilson Rawls was born on September 24, 1913, in Scraper, Oklahoma. Scraper is a very small town in the middle of the Ozarks region. The Ozarks cover a big area in the south-central part of the United States. How big? About 50,000 square miles! The Ozarks include parts of four states: Arkansas, Kansas, Missouri, and Oklahoma. The Ozarks are surrounded by rivers. If you look on a map, the north (top) of the Ozarks is bordered by the Missouri River. The south (bottom) is the Arkansas River. The east (right) is bounded by the Mississippi River. The west (left) is stopped by the Grand and Neosho rivers. The Ozarks are a beautiful area that is filled with trails, streams, and grand mountains.

Since Rawls's mother, Winnie Hatfield Rawls, was part Cherokee Indian, she had been given some land in Oklahoma by the federal government. (The United States gave land to some Native Americans who had been displaced from their original land.) Winnie and her husband, Minzy, farmed the land and raised their children on it.

In the spring, the family woke up to the rich smell of the earth after a gentle rain. The birds chirped and the leaves swayed in the breeze. In the winter, the family shivered in the chilly wind and crackly frost. No matter what season, the day started and ended with chores: milking the cows, feeding the pigs, hoeing the crops. The family's vegetables came from their fields. Their meat came from the woods, not the supermarket: The Rawls family trapped and ate squirrels, raccoons, bears, and rabbits.

Rawls's hunting dog was not only his best friend but also a way to help his parents earn enough money to survive. Rawls and his father sold the fur skins from the animals they trapped. These skins, called pelts, were made into warm coats, hats, and mittens. The family used the money they earned from the pelts to buy things they needed that they couldn't grow or hunt. It was a hard life, but one filled with love of nature, family, and God.

Nearly everyone in the Ozarks was poor. Like the Rawls family, they lived off the land and just got by. In 1929 the New York stock market crashed. How could something that happened in

New York City—way across the United States—affect people in the Ozarks? The stock market crash affected people all around the world.

Almost overnight, the world plunged into the Great Depression. Companies did not have the money to pay their workers, so many people lost their jobs. Companies could not hire new workers, either. As a result, it became almost impossible to find a job. By 1933 one quarter of all workers were unemployed: About 13 million people did not have jobs. Because there were so few jobs, people took whatever work they could find. Like most other people at this time, the Rawls family did not have enough money to buy food and clothing. In 1929, when he was sixteen years old, Wilson Rawls left home and traveled all over the country looking for any work he could do. He wanted to support himself and be able to send some money home for his family, too.

At first, he worked as a carpenter and a handyman. Then he worked on construction jobs all over the world, including Mexico and South America. He helped build the Alcan Highway in Alaska and five major dams in the United States. He labored in West Coast shipyards, for the Navy in Oregon, and for a lumber company in Canada.

No matter where he was, Rawls kept on writing. His arms may have hurt from hammering all day, but he stayed up late writing. Unfortunately, he did not know much about grammar and spelling, so his stories had lots of writing mistakes. As a result, no one would buy them. The rejections made him sad, but it was his lack of learning that depressed him. Nevertheless, Rawls saved his stories in an old trunk.

In 1957 Rawls went north to Idaho. There, when he was working for the Atomic Energy Commission, he met Sophie Styczinski. They fell in love! A year later, they got married and were very happy together. Sophie helped Rawls with his writing by fixing his spelling, capitalization, and punctuation mistakes.

In 1961 Rawls published *Where the Red Fern Grows*. All his hard work and determination had paid off. In 1976 he wrote one more book, *The Summer of the Monkeys*. Just like *Where the Red Fern Grows*, *The Summer of the Monkeys* has become a classic.

Wilson Rawls died in 1984, but his novels live on in the hearts of children and adults around the world.

> "The sweetest music I have ever heard is the snake-like buzz of a busy reel, and there is no feeling like the feel of a trusted rod bent in a rainbow arch by a fighting trout on the end of a line."
>
> —Wilson Rawls

"**W**rite what you know best!" is the advice often given to beginning writers. Wilson Rawls did just that. He wrote about his childhood, when he hunted for raccoons with his loyal dogs. He described the hot, dusty summers and the fierce winter blizzards in Oklahoma. He told of his love for his parents and sisters, too. He explained how much loyalty and God meant to him. He wrote all about his life as a young boy: the joy and the sorrow, the good times and the bad times. The result is *Where the Red Fern Grows*. The novel is the real-life story of Rawls's childhood.

Since there weren't any schools in the area, Rawls's mother taught her children at home. She read aloud from books she had ordered through the mail. You've probably read many of the stories that Rawls heard from his mother: *The Little Red Hen*, *The Three Little Pigs*, and *Little Red Riding Hood*.

At first young "Woody" didn't like the books. "I thought all books were . . . GIRL stories!" he said. "Then one day Mama brought home a book that changed my life. It was a story about a man and a dog—Jack London's *Call of the Wild*." The book influenced Rawls to become a writer. He explained it this way: "After we finished reading the book, Mama gave it to me. It was my first real treasure and I carried it with me wherever I went and read it every chance I got." He even read the book aloud to his dog!

Wilson Rawls had found his goal: When he grew up, he wanted to be a writer. He wanted to write a story about a boy and a dog that would affect others as much as *The Call of the Wild* had affected him. He wanted to touch his readers' hearts as well as their minds.

As you read earlier, Rawls kept writing and writing but had no luck selling the story of his childhood. Just a few weeks before his wedding, he decided to give up his dream of being a writer. He felt that as a married man, it was time to be responsible. On a hot August day, Rawls took all his stories out of the old trunk and burned them. He burned five stories—including *Where the Red Fern Grows*!

Deep inside, though, Rawls still wanted to be a writer, so he told Sophie how he had burned his manuscripts. He told her how Jack London's novel *The Call of the Wild* had sparked his desire to write adventure stories. He described the long nights he had spent writing stories by a campfire at the side of the road.

Sophie felt sad because she believed that Wilson should have a chance to make his dream come true. She persuaded him to rewrite the story of the boy and his two hunting dogs. It had taken Rawls twenty years to write *Where the Red Fern Grows* the first time. Luckily, it took him only three weeks to rewrite it! Sophie helped Wilson fix many of his spelling and grammar mistakes. In 1961 Wilson and Sophie sold the book to a very popular magazine, *The Saturday Evening Post*.

For three months, *The Saturday Evening Post* published chapters from *Where the Red Fern Grows*. The *Post* called the story "The Hounds of Youth." People loved it! Later that year, *Where the Red Fern Grows* was published as a book. Rawls's dream of being a writer had come true.

Chapter Charter:
Questions to Guide Your Reading

Chapter 1
- Who is telling the story? When do you think the events take place?
- The narrator helps the old redbone hound. Have you or anyone in your family ever helped a stray animal? If so, when and why?
- What memories does the old dog stir in the narrator?

Chapter 2
- In what way does the action change? How can you tell?
- Billy wants a pair of hunting dogs. Have you ever wanted anything as much as Billy wants these dogs? If so, what was it and did you get it?
- Would you like to be friends with Billy? Why or why not?

Chapter 3
- What is Billy's plan to get his coonhounds? Do you think it will work? Why or why not?
- Why do you think Billy's grandfather helps him get the hounds?
- What might it feel like to work for two years to achieve your dream?

Chapter 4

- Billy walks about forty miles to pick up his puppies. Would you have gone to pick up the puppies yourself or waited for them to be delivered? Explain your answer.
- How do you think Billy feels as he walks through the town of Tahlequah?
- Why are the people in Tahlequah so cruel to Billy?

Chapter 5

- How does Billy feel when he first sees his hounds?
- Do you think Billy should have fought back when the kids teased and attacked him? Why or why not?
- Why do you think the marshal helps Billy?

Chapter 6

- What is special about the way Billy finally names his puppies? What does this scene tell you about Billy's beliefs?
- Why do you think Billy is so happy to buy gifts for his family?
- Why do Billy's parents want to move to town? Would you rather live in a small village or a big city? Explain your reasons.

Chapter 7

- Have you ever trained a pet? If so, how did you do it? If not, how do you think you might go about training an animal?
- Do you think you would be able to trap a coon as Billy does? Why or why not?
- Why does Papa make Billy take down all his traps? Do you agree with Papa's decision? Why or why not?

Chapter 8

- How does Billy feel when hunting season opens? What events in your life make you feel the same way?
- What is your first clue that Little Ann and Old Dan are great hunting dogs?
- When the dogs trap the raccoon in the old sycamore tree, Billy cuts "the giant" down. Do you agree with his decision? Why or why not?

Chapter 9

- Why is Billy so determined to cut down the tree and get the raccoon? When did you last feel as determined as Billy does to achieve a difficult task?
- How would you describe the relationship between Old Dan and Little Ann?
- Billy describes killing the coon as "savage and brutal." Do you think people should hunt animals? Why or why not?

Chapter 10

- Why do you think Billy is such a successful raccoon hunter?
- How would you feel if you were Billy, catching so many raccoons?
- Old Dan and Little Ann are clever, determined dogs. What experiences have you had with smart, loyal animals?

Chapter 11

- How does Billy rescue Little Ann after her accident? What does this tell you about Billy's character?
- Would you have rescued Little Ann if you had been in Billy's shoes? Why or why not?
- How can you tell that Billy is very religious?

Chapter 12

- Would you like to be friends with the Pritchards? Why or why not?
- Do you agree with Billy's decision not to tell his parents about his plans to hunt with Rainie and Rubin? Explain your answer. Would you have told *your* parents?
- Who do you predict will win the bet, Billy or the Pritchards? Why?

Chapter 13

- Do you agree with Billy's decision not to kill the ghost coon? Why or why not?
- Explain how Rubin gets killed. How did his death make you feel?
- How can you tell that Billy is compassionate, kind, and respectful?

Chapter 14

- What event would make you feel as happy as Billy feels about entering the championship coon hunt? Why?
- Who do you think is more excited about the championship coon hunt, Billy or Grandpa? Why?
- What clues from Chapter 1 suggest that Billy will win the championship hunt?

Chapter 15

- What qualities do Little Ann and Old Dan have that make them such great hunting dogs?
- How would you feel if you were Billy, with so much riding on this contest?

- Imagine that you were one of the judges. Would you have awarded Little Ann first prize in the contest? Give your reasons.

Chapter 16
- Is the contest fair to the hunters, dogs, and raccoons? Why or why not?
- Why are raccoons so hard to hunt?
- Imagine you were Billy. How would you feel at the end of this day?

Chapter 17
- In what way does the weather become a character in this chapter?
- Imagine that you were hunting with Billy. Would you have turned back at this point? Why or why not?
- In what ways are Billy and Grandpa alike here?

Chapter 18
- How do you think Billy feels when he sees Little Ann and Old Dan covered in ice?
- Mr. Kyle says, "You can read every day where a dog saved the life of a drowning child, or lay down his life for his master. Some people call this loyalty. I don't. I may be wrong, but I call it love—the deepest kind of love." Do you think the dogs are showing loyalty or love? Explain your answer.
- What do you think Mama and Papa will do with the three hundred dollars that Billy wins?

Chapter 19

- Why do you think Old Dan attacks the mountain lion?
- Imagine you were Billy. If you could relive the scene with the mountain lion, what would you do differently? What would you do the same?
- Old Dan and Little Ann die within a short time of each other. How did their deaths make you feel?

Chapter 20

- How does the family feel about leaving the Ozarks?
- What is the legend of the red fern?
- How can you tell that Billy has come to accept the death of his beloved dogs?

Plot: What's Happening?

"I suppose there's a time in practically every young boy's life when he's affected by that wonderful disease of puppy love."

—Billy, *Where the Red Fern Grows*

Where the Red Fern Grows is the story of a boy's love for his two hunting dogs. It's also about life in the rural Ozark mountains in the early part of this century, about family, love, and faith.

The story is told by Billy Colman, now an adult. On the way home from work, Billy breaks up a savage dogfight. He rescues the old redbone hound the other dogs were attacking. The dog makes Billy remember his childhood. The next night, after letting the redbone hound go free, Billy thinks about the two red hunting dogs he had as a child. He remembers how much they meant to him.

Then the story flashes back to the past. Billy is still telling the story, but now he is ten years old. Billy, his parents, and his younger sisters live on a farm in the Ozark Mountains in Oklahoma. Have you ever wanted something so badly that it's more important than food and sleep? That's how Billy feels about hunting dogs. He wants two coonhounds more than anything else in the world, but his papa does not have enough money to buy them. It is the Great Depression and Billy's family, like so many other families, is very poor.

Billy works small jobs for two years and saves up the money to buy the hounds. Only then does he tell his plan to his grandpa, who helps arrange the purchase. Months later, the dogs arrive at the train depot at Tahlequah, more than twenty miles away. Billy is too excited to wait a week for a ride. What does he do? He walks there! Billy takes some food and sneaks out of the house at night without telling anyone his plan.

In Tahlequah, grown-ups as well as kids make fun of Billy because his clothes are patched and he is barefoot. Since the puppies cost less than advertised, Billy has money left over. Because he is generous, he buys nice gifts for his family.

The kindly stationmaster gives Billy his puppies. Billy holds them and cries. He walks through town with the puppies in his sack as people stare and laugh at him. A gang of kids beats up Billy and hurts his puppies. The town marshal breaks up the mob and helps Billy brush off. He gains respect for Billy when he learns how long he worked for the pups. He buys Billy his first bottle of soda pop.

On his long walk home, Billy names the male puppy Old Dan and the female puppy Little Ann. Back at home, Billy gives his family the gifts he bought and tells everyone about his adventures.

During the summer and fall, Billy teaches his hounds how to hunt raccoons. The dogs are quick learners. They make a great team: No raccoon can outsmart Little Ann, and Old Dan is strong and sure. More than that, the dogs are loyal to each other and to Billy.

The dogs trap their first raccoon in a huge sycamore tree. Billy spends days cutting down the tree. When it finally topples over, the coon runs out, and the dogs attack. Billy returns home happily. He believes that God helped him by sending a wind to help knock down the tree.

Billy hunts every night and traps many coons. Grandpa helps him sell the skins. Billy and the dogs have many exciting adventures. During one adventure, Little Ann falls into the icy river and almost dies. Billy saves her.

One day, the cruel Pritchard boys, Rubin and Rainie, bet Billy that his dogs can't "tree" (trap in a tree) the "ghost coon." On the hunt, Rubin accidentally falls on Billy's ax as he tries to kill Billy's dogs. Rubin dies and Billy is very sad.

To make Billy feel better, Grandpa enters him and his dogs in a big coon hunt. Billy, Grandpa, and Papa go to the competition. On the first day, Little Ann wins as the best-looking dog and gets a silver cup.

Billy qualifies for the championship round in which his dogs kill three coons. As Billy hunts, a fierce blizzard strikes. Billy can't find his dogs in the blinding snow! He finally locates the half-frozen dogs circling a treed coon. When they kill the fourth coon, Billy wins the championship and the three-hundred-dollar jackpot. The rescue party finds Billy, Papa, Grandpa, and the hunters with them. Billy cries when he gets the gold cup. Back home, Billy gives the three hundred dollars to his parents and the gold and silver cups to his sisters.

Soon after, a mountain lion attacks Old Dan and Little Ann. Old Dan dies of his injuries. Two days later, Little Ann loses the will to live and dies. Billy buries her beside Old Dan.

With Billy's prize money and the money he made from selling coonskins, the family moves to town in the spring. There, the children can go to school.

On the day they move, Billy goes to his dogs' graves to say good-bye. He finds a tall, beautiful red fern between the graves. He remembers the Indian legend about a little boy and girl who had been lost in a blizzard and had frozen to death. When their bodies were found in the spring, a red fern had grown between them. According to the legend, only an angel can plant a red fern, which never dies and makes the spot holy. The adult Billy thinks that he would like to go back to his home in the Ozarks. He is sure the red fern is still there.

Thinking about the plot
• How does Billy finally get his puppies?
• Why are the dogs so important to Billy? to his family?
• What part of the story did you find the most exciting? Why?

"Papa said, 'I intend to butcher a hog.
We're about out of meat.' Looking at
me, he said, 'Shell a sack of corn. Take
one of the mules and go to the mill for
your mother.'"

—*Where the Red Fern Grows*

Time: When does the story take place?

Where the Red Fern Grows takes place in the early 1930s. At that
time, the world was in the longest and worst economic crisis in
modern times. This crisis was called the Great Depression. It
started with the stock market crash on October 29, 1929, and
did not end until the early 1940s. Stores, companies, and banks
went out of business. People lost their jobs, homes, and savings.

Where the Red Fern Grows takes place around 1933, the worst
year of the Depression. That year, more than one quarter of all
workers did not have jobs. People patched their clothes and went
without new things. In big cities, the jobless sold apples and
shined shoes on street corners to earn a little money. Many
people needed charity to survive. Some people searched garbage
dumps for food or ate grass and weeds. In small towns, people

ate what they could grow, hunt, or find. People often went to bed hungry.

In the 1930s nearly everyone in the Ozarks was poor. Rawls suggests the deep poverty in this area by describing how Papa cannot afford to buy Billy his hunting dogs, even though the family could use the pelts and meat they would bring. Papa explains it to Billy this way:

> He told me how hard times were, and that it looked like a man couldn't get a fair price for anything he raised. Some of the farmers had quit farming and were cutting railroad ties so they could feed their families. If things didn't get better, that's what he'd have to do. He said he'd give anything if he could get some good hounds for me, but there didn't seem to be any way he could right then.

The family can't afford to buy clothing, although their clothes are ragged. Billy does not have shoes. His feet are all cut up. "I took one look at my bare feet and winced," he says. "They were as brown as dead sycamore leaves. The spider-web pattern of raw, red patches looked odd in the saddle-brown skin."

Mama starts crying when Billy brings her some fabric for a new dress. It has been a long time since Mama and the girls have had any new clothing. "The light that was shining from my mother's eyes, as she fingered the cheap cotton cloth, was something I will never forget," Billy says to the reader.

Place: Where are we?

Take a giant step back in time to Oklahoma in the 1930s. Hungry for meat? If so, you have to hunt it or raise it yourself. As you read in the quote at the beginning of this chapter, Pa must butcher a pig to get food for the family. The family raises chickens for meat and eggs. They also eat the raccoons and squirrels that Billy hunts. They catch and eat fish, too. Since there is no electricity or refrigeration, the family smokes, salts, and dries their meat to preserve it. Billy takes a slab of salt pork with him to eat when he goes to pick up his puppies.

The family grows their own vegetables, picks wild berries in the woods, and finds honey in hollow logs. To get cornmeal, they grow corn, pick it, and clean it. They "shell" the ears of the corn by cutting off all the kernels. These kernels are dried and then ground into cornmeal at the mill. The miller takes some of the cornmeal as his pay. The family uses the rest of it to make corn bread, corn muffins, and corn cakes.

After Billy wins the hunting championship, the family has a big, fancy meal. "Papa went to the smokehouse and came back with a hickory-cured ham. We sat down to a feast of the ham, huge plates of fried potatoes, ham gravy, hot corn bread, fresh butter, and wild bee honey." At that time, there wasn't any take-out food, frozen food, or microwave food!

Rural Oklahoma in the 1930s is a place without many cars. People walk to get places: the fields, their friends' farms, and the few stores in town. If you have a heavy sack of cornmeal to carry, you put it on a mule, just as Billy does. People often walk long, long distances. Billy walks about forty miles round trip to Tahlequah to pick up his puppies.

Rural Oklahoma in the 1930s is also a place without much indoor plumbing. Since there's no water inside the house, taking a bath is a long process. First, you have to get water from the outside well and carry it inside. Then you heat the water on the wood stove. (Don't forget to chop the wood for the stove fire!) Next, you (or your parents) have to pour the water carefully into a big copper tub. Finally, you can take your bath. But since it is so hard to set up the bath, no one wastes the hot water. After you have your bath, your brothers and sisters take turns in the same water. It's no wonder most people bathed only once a week!

Few home have electric lights. There is no television, no video games, no washing machines, no computers, no hair dryers, no microwaves, and no air-conditioning. Only a few people have telephones. People may know what an airplane is, but it is unlikely that anyone in this area has actually seen one.

Life is hard in Oklahoma in the 1930s, but it is also beautiful. Billy loves the land. "I had never seen a night so peaceful and still," he says the first night he hunts alone. "All around me tall sycamores gleamed like white streamers in the moonlight." Billy especially likes the biggest tree in the forest. It is so big that he calls it "the giant." Billy likes to lie on the ground in the warm sun and stare at its leafy branches.

Most of all, Billy likes to run through the woods with his dogs and hunt raccoons. "What wonderful nights they were," he says, "running like a deer through the thick timber of the bottoms, tearing my way through stands of wild cane, climbing over drifts, and jumping logs, running, and screaming, and yelling, 'Who-e-e-e, get him, boy, get him,' following the voices of my little hounds."

Oklahoma in the 1930s is a place of death as well as beauty. Animals and people kill and eat other animals to live. One night in the woods, Billy hears this happen: "I heard a sharp snap and a feathery rustle in some brush close by. A small rodent started squealing in agony. A night hawk had found its supper." Billy, too, must hunt for food.

Deadly storms flatten crops and can even kill people. Billy and the other hunters get trapped in a terrible blizzard. "The wind-driven sleet stung our skin like thousands of pricking needles. Strong gusts of wind growled and moaned through the tops of the tall timber," Billy says. Grandpa falls on the icy ground and hurts his leg. If Little Ann had not found him, he would have frozen to death.

Later in the book, a fierce mountain lion tries to attack Billy. "There was a low cough and a deep growl from the lion. I saw him crouch. I knew what was coming. My hands felt hot and sweaty on the smooth ash handle of the ax. With a blood-curdling scream, he sprang from the tree with claws outspread and long, yellow fangs bared." Billy's dogs bravely fight the mountain lion.

Sadly, Old Dan dies from his injuries. Little Ann dies shortly after, too sad to go on without Old Dan.

Thinking about the setting

- When and where does *Where the Red Fern Grows* take place?
- How does Rawls use description to make you feel as if you are with Billy and his family?
- How is life different for Billy than it is for you? How is it the same?

Themes/Layers of Meaning: Is That What It *Really* Means?

"Two beautiful cups gleamed from the mantel. I held the match up so I could get a better look. There they were, sitting side by side....There was a story in those cups—a story that went back more than a half century."

—Billy, *Where the Red Fern Grows*

The theme of a literary work is its main idea. It is a general statement about life. The quotation you just read suggests the main themes of *Where the Red Fern Grows*: determination, sacrifice, and love. There are a few other themes as well, because a good story like this one makes us think about life in many different ways. Let's look at the themes in *Where the Red Fern Grows*.

Determination pays off

Billy is determined. People who are determined set goals and work until they reach them. We can see how determined Billy is from the beginning of his story. He wants a pair of hunting dogs more than anything else in the world, but his papa does not have the money to buy them. The puppies cost fifty dollars. Today, fifty dollars isn't a fortune, but it sure was in the 1930s.

Billy shows his determination by working for two years to save enough money to buy the hounds. "Slowly a plan began to form," he thinks. "I'd save the money. I could sell stuff to the fishermen: crawfish, minnows, and fresh vegetables. In berry season, I could sell all the berries I could pick at my grandfather's store. I could trap in the winter. . . . There was the way to get those pups—save my money." Penny by penny, nickel by nickel, Billy saves the money. His determination pays off and he is able to buy the puppies. They cost ten dollars less than he expected, but he still saved the entire fifty dollars.

The marshal in Tahlequah is very impressed with Billy's determination. After he breaks up the fight and helps Billy, the marshal asks Billy about his puppies:

> Walking over, he knelt down and started petting the pups. "They're fine-looking dogs," he said. "Where did you get them?"
>
> I told him I had ordered them from Kentucky.
>
> "What did they cost you?" he asked.
>
> "Forty dollars," I said.
>
> He asked if my father had bought them for me.
>
> "No," I said. "I bought them myself."
>
> He asked me where I got the money.

"I worked and saved it," I said.

"It takes a long time to save forty dollars," he said.

"Yes," I said. "It took me two years."

"Two years!" he exclaimed.

I saw an outraged look come over the marshal's face. Reaching up, he pushed his hat back. He glanced up and down the street. I heard him mutter, "There's not one in that bunch with that kind of grit."

The marshal admires Billy's determination, which he calls "grit." The marshal knows that the kids who picked on Billy don't have that kind of determination. They don't work for what they want.

Billy's dogs, Old Dan and Little Ann, are just as determined as Billy is. That's one reason why Billy and his dogs are such a good team. Little Ann always sticks to a raccoon's trail, and Old Dan never gives up the chase. The hounds stay with the coons they chase up a tree even when they might die. During the big hunt competition, for example, Old Dan and Little Ann stay with the last raccoon in the blizzard—even though they get covered in ice. Mr. Benson says: "Those two hounds. I found them. They're frozen solid. They're nothing but white ice from the tips of their noses to the ends of their tails." Mr. Benson is wrong: The dogs are not frozen solid. Billy is able thaw the ice from their bodies and they are not hurt. Because they are determined and stay with the coon, Billy wins the competition.

Many people praise the dogs for their determination. Old Dan is determined until the very end of his life. We see this when Billy has to pry Old Dan's jaws from the mountain lion. Little Ann loses her determination after Old Dan dies, but this is because the dogs were a team.

Determination pays off for Billy and his dogs. With his dogs, Billy is able to earn money to help his family. Billy also has a lot of fun hunting with his dogs. From their example, we can see that Rawls believes that determination helps people achieve their goals and have a happier life.

The importance of sacrifice

Sacrifice is another theme in *Where the Red Fern Grows*. From the actions of Billy, his family, and his dogs, you can figure out that Rawls believes that people should sacrifice for other people. When you sacrifice, you give up something to help someone else. You might give up time, money, or an object you value, for example. True sacrifices are given freely, with love and affection. We see many examples of selfless sacrifice in the novel. Often, one sacrifice leads to another.

Every time Grandpa gives Billy candy, for instance, Billy gives it to his sisters. Billy loves candy and he rarely gets any. Therefore, you would think that he would want to keep it, but he doesn't. He wants to make his sisters happy. When Billy has ten dollars left over from buying the puppies, he spends the money on gifts for his parents and sisters. He does not spend the money on himself, even though he wants a hunting rifle very much.

Billy learns the importance of sacrifice from his parents. Billy's father often helps Billy hunt, even though Mr. Colman needs the time to take care of the animals and farm. Billy's sisters sacrifice their time, too. Billy says, "With the help of my oldest sister, we started giving my pups their first lessons. She would hold their collars while I made trails with the hide for them to follow." Billy's little sister brings him lunch when he is cutting down the big sycamore tree. "When my sister came with the lunch bucket," Billy says, "I could have kissed her." Grandpa drives into the woods to help Billy with the tree, too. Grandpa teaches Billy how to make a stuffed man to fool the coon into staying in the tree.

Old Dan and Little Ann make the biggest sacrifice in the book. Old Dan sacrifices his life for Billy in the fight against the mountain lion. Billy says: "I never saw my dogs when they got between the lion and me, but they were there. Side by side, they rose up from the ground at once. They sailed straight into those jaws of death, their small, red bodies taking the ripping, slashing claws meant for me."

The strength of love

Billy's family is very close and loving. Mama makes Billy a hat with the pelt from the first raccoon he catches. This shows that she support his hunting and is happy that he is happy. Mama comforts Billy when he is tired, frightened, or sad. Billy's family helps one another in good times and bad times. Their love helps them get through the hardest times of all, the poverty and despair of the Great Depression.

Billy is very close to his grandpa, who teaches him all he knows about coon hunting. Grandpa is also Billy's greatest hunting supporter. When Grandpa enters Old Dan and Little Ann in the big hunting contest, Billy is thrilled. He says: "I was so surprised at what Grandpa had said that I couldn't utter a word. At first I was scared and then a wonderful feeling came over me. I felt the excitement of the big hunt as it burned its way through my body, I started breathing like I had been running for a hundred miles." Even when Grandpa is badly hurt, he stands by Billy. He will not leave the hunting grounds until Billy gets his prize. "Snorting and growling, Grandpa said, 'I told you I wasn't going anywhere till I see the gold cup handed to this boy.'"

Billy and his dogs love one another, too. One of the hunters says that Billy's hounds seem to have more than just loyalty for him. They also love him deeply. "My whole life was wrapped up in my dogs," Billy tells the reader.

The power of spirituality

Billy believes in a higher power. When the big sycamore finally falls over, Billy believes that it was guided by God. Billy asks his parents about the event. Billy says to his father:

"I thought something strange happened down at the bottoms this afternoon."...

I told him about how my hands had gotten so sore I couldn't chop any more, and how I had asked for strength to finish the job.

"Well, what's so strange about that?" he asked.

"I don't know," I said, "but I didn't chop the big tree down. The wind blew it over.". . .

"It wasn't just the wind," I said. "It was the way it blew. It didn't touch another tree in the bottoms. . . . Do you think God heard my prayer? Do you think He helped me?". . .

"I don't know, Billy. I'm afraid I can't answer that. . . . No, I'm afraid I can't help you there. You have to decide for yourself."

It wasn't hard for me to decide. I was firmly convinced that I had been helped.

Throughout the novel, Billy prays when times get tough. It seems to Billy that his prayers are answered. However, his faith is shaken when his dogs die. He cannot understand why Old Dan and Little Ann had to die. Perhaps the dogs died to help other creatures. By killing the mountain lion the dogs have gotten rid of a terrible threat in the forest.

After the dogs die, a red fern grows over their grave. Billy knows the story of the fern:

I had heard the old Indian legend about the red fern. How a little Indian boy and girl were lost in a blizzard and had frozen to death. In the spring, when they were found, a beautiful red fern had grown up between their bodies. The story went on to say that only an angel could plant the seeds of a red fern, and that they never died; where one grew, that spot was sacred.

When he sees the fern, Billy's faith comes back to him. He believes that his dogs had a holy purpose on earth. His belief in a spiritual power helps Billy accept their deaths.

Thinking about the themes

- One of the hunters says: "You can read every day where a dog saved the life of a drowning child, or lay down his life for his master. Some people call this loyalty. I don't. I may be wrong, but I call it love—the deepest kind of love." Based on what you read in *Where the Red Fern Grows*, do you agree? Why or why not?
- What was the last goal you worked to achieve? How did your determination help you?
- Arrange the themes in this section in order from most to least important to you.

Characters: Who Are These People, Anyway?

"Mama was the best helper a boy ever had."

—Billy, *Where the Red Fern Grows*

Where the Red Fern Grows has three main characters: Billy Colman and his two hunting dogs, Old Dan and Little Ann. Below is a list of all the characters. After you read the list, read on to find out more about some of the important characters in the novel.

The Colmans

Billy Colman	ten-year-old narrator
Papa Colman	Billy's father, a farmer
Mama Colman	Billy's mother
the girls	Billy's three younger sisters, never named
Grandpa	Billy's grandfather, a storekeeper
Grandma	Billy's grandmother

Animals

Little Ann	Billy's female hunting hound
Old Dan	Billy's male hunting hound
mountain lion	fierce creature who attacks Billy

| ghost coon | sneaky old raccoon |
| Samie | the Colmans' cat |

Other Characters

Rainie Pritchard	ten-year-old neighbor boy
Rubin Pritchard	twelve-year-old neighbor boy
Mrs. Pritchard	Rainie and Rubin's mother
Mr. Pritchard	Rainie and Rubin's father
Mr. Benson	one of the hunters
Mr. Kyle	one of the hunters
the marshal	sheriff of Tahlequah
the stationmaster	stationmaster of Tahlequah depot

Billy Colman: Billy is not only the novel's main character but also its narrator. Everything we learn in the book comes through Billy's eyes.

Ten-year-old Billy is strong, brave, and hardworking. He says, "I had the wind of a deer, the muscles of a country boy, a heart full of dog love, and a strong determination. I wasn't scared of the darkness, or the mountains, for I was raised in those mountains."

Billy doesn't care about the way he looks. He doesn't pay any attention to his clothes or hair. When he is in town picking up his puppies, Billy sees his full reflection for the first time in his life. He is surprised at what he sees: "My straw-colored hair was long and shaggy, and was brushed out like a corn tassel that had been hit by the wind. . . . My overalls were patched and faded but they were clean. My shirt had pulled out. . . . I pumped up one of my arms and thought surely the muscle was going to pop right through my thin blue shirt."

Billy loves his parents and sisters, but he loves his dogs and raccoon hunting more than anything else. "I was a hunter from the time I could walk," he says. "I caught lizards on the rail fences, rats in the corncrib, and frogs in the little creek that ran through the fields." Although Billy is a great coon hunter, he cares more about his dogs than about catching a lot of raccoons. Billy loves his dogs and takes good care of them.

From the very beginning of the book, we can see that Billy is kind and generous. When Grandpa gives Billy a bag of candy, Billy takes a few pieces and saves the rest for his sisters. "Arriving home," Billy says, "I dumped the sack of candy out on the bed. Six little hands helped themselves. I was well repaid by the love and adoration I saw in the wide blue eyes of my three little sisters." Later in the novel, Billy gives his three-hundred-dollar contest winnings to his parents.

Billy is also deeply religious. For example, he believes that his dogs have been sent by heaven. Billy says: "Just when I had given up all hope of ever owning a good hound, something wonderful happened. The good Lord figured I had hurt enough, and it was time to lend a helping hand." When his dogs die, Billy believes they have gone to heaven. Billy says: "Good-bye, Old Dan and Little Ann. I'll never forget you; and this I know—if God made room in heaven for all good dogs, I know He made a special place for you."

Little Ann and Old Dan: These are Billy's dogs. They are special hunting dogs—just the kind of dogs that Billy wants. "I didn't just want one dog," he says. "I wanted two, and not just any kind of a dog. They had to be a special kind and a special breed." These special hunting dogs are called hounds.

There are many different kinds of hounds: wolfhounds, deerhounds, coonhounds, and foxhounds, for example. Each kind of hound hunts the animal in its name. Wolfhounds hunt wolves, deerhounds hunt deer, coonhounds hunt raccoons, and so on.

Coonhounds are born wanting to hunt raccoons. They hunt by following the animal's smell. Little Ann and Old Dan are called "redbone" coonhounds because they are a deep red color. When redbone coonhounds track raccoons, their tail goes up in the air and their ears drag on the ground. These dogs also make good family pets.

Little Ann is Billy's female hound. She is very small for her type of dog. However, Little Ann more than makes up for her small size with her great intelligence. Billy says: "I didn't have to look twice to see that what she lacked in power, she made up in brains. She was a much smarter dog than the boy dog, more sure of herself, more cautious. I knew that when the trail became tough, she would be the one to unravel it." Sure enough, no raccoon can trick Little Ann! She loves Billy and Old Dan. Billy tells his mother, "Did you know, Mama, that Little Ann used to come every night and peek in my window just to see if I was all right?" Little Ann is very loyal to Old Dan. She stays by Old Dan's side no matter what happens. When Old Dan dies, Little Ann lays her head on his grave. "With the last ounce of strength in her body, she had dragged herself to the grave of Old Dan." She dies on his grave.

Old Dan is Billy's male hound. Old Dan is strong, brave, and determined. He will hunt with only Billy and Little Ann, and he never gives up a chase. Mama and Papa are amazed at Old Dan's spirit. After Old Dan sleeps in the woods all night to keep a raccoon in the big sycamore tree, Mama says, "Well, I never in all my life. I had no idea a dog loved to hunt that much." When Old Dan kills the mountain lion, Billy has to pry his locked jaws apart with the ax handle. "I led him off to one side," Billy says. "I couldn't turn him loose as I knew if I did, he would go back to the lion."

Grandpa: Billy's grandpa runs a store. Grandpa and Billy love each other very much. Billy admires his grandfather, too. Billy says, "I had the finest grandpa in the world." Readers see how much Billy loves his grandpa during the championship hunt. When Grandpa is lost in the storm at the end of the hunt, Billy says: "I couldn't hold back the tears. My grandfather was lost and wandering in that white jungle of cane. Screaming for him, I started back." Billy is very relieved when Grandpa is found, suffering only a minor injury.

Grandpa helps Billy make his dream of hunting raccoons come true. First, Grandpa helps Billy earn money to buy the hounds. Grandpa does this by buying and selling the berries that Billy picks. Then Grandpa writes the order letters for the purchase of the hounds. Later, Grandpa enters the dogs in the championship coon hunt. Grandpa likes to tell jokes and exaggerated stories about Old Dan and Little Ann. If the dogs caught two coons, Grandpa says they caught five!

Papa: Billy's papa is a good man who always tries to do what is right. For example, he makes Billy take down the traps that hurt the raccoons. Papa says: "I don't think this is very sportsmanlike. The coon doesn't have a chance. It's all right this time. You needed this one, but from now on I want you to catch them with your dogs. That way they have a fifty-fifty chance."

Papa understands that Billy is growing up and needs to do things on his own. For example, Papa lets Billy go hunting alone and cut down the giant tree by himself. Papa lets Billy hunt in the snow and ice, too. Papa wants the best for Billy and his sisters. At the end of the story, Papa and Mama move to town so their children can go to school.

Mama: Billy's mama is a hardworking, religious, and kind woman. She loves Billy very much and worries that he will get hurt while hunting. However, Mama understands how important hunting and the hounds are to Billy. As a result, she tries to help him as much as she can. She encourages Papa to go with Billy on the hunt. "Why, don't you worry about the girls and me," Mama said. "We'll be all right. Besides, it'll be several months yet before I need any help." That's when Billy realizes that Mama is going to have a baby. It can be dangerous for a pregnant woman to be alone far away from a town, but Mama wants Billy to have his chance to hunt in the big contest. That's why she encourages him to go.

Billy and his mother are close to each other. They can talk about important issues. Billy often has serious talks with his mother about life, death, and heaven. When Old Dan and Little Ann die, Billy goes to his mother for comfort. He asks her if God made a special place for dogs in heaven. She says: "From what I've read in the Good Book, Billy, He put far more things up there than we have here. Yes, I'm sure He did." Mama's words make Billy feel much better.

Thinking about the characters
• What do you like the most about Billy?
• How does the author show us that Mr. and Mrs. Colman are good parents?
• *Where the Red Fern Grows* is based on the true story of Wilson Rawls's childhood. Which characters seem the most true to life? Why?

"The book is a heart warming classic for all ages."

—David Nishimoto, North Ogden, Utah

Remember how Wilson Rawls burned the manuscript for *Where the Red Fern Grows*? Rawls was so sad that no one wanted to publish his writing that he began to think that he did not have talent. Talking about his book years later, Rawls told the *Salt Lake Tribune:* "I was sure it was pure trash. I was sure that no one would waste time printing junk like that. I also knew my grammar was poor and my vocabulary was zero." The book *did* get published. However, *Where the Red Fern Grows* wasn't an instant best-seller. Far from it!

At first, the book sold v-e-r-y slowly. "*Where the Red Fern Grows* didn't sell a dozen copies for the first seven years," Rawls claims, "then a miracle came along." The "miracle" happened when he was invited to speak at a teachers' workshop on children's books at the University of Utah. The teachers liked his talk and his book, and began telling their students about it. "That was the spark," Rawls said, "and the book has been selling ever since." And now it *is* a best-seller!

Soon, critics noticed the book. They saw its charm and the author's talent. As a result, *Where the Red Fern Grows* has earned many of the top awards given in children's literature. In 1979 the novel won the Sequoyah Children's Book Award, given by the Oklahoma Library Association. That same year, it won the William Allen White Children's Book Award, given by Emporia State University. There's more! In 1979 the novel also won the Evansville (Illinois) Book Award from the Vanderburgh School Corporation. The following year, it won the Golden Archer Award from the University of Wisconsin–Oshkosh. In 1980 *Where the Red Fern Grows* won the Maud Hart Lovelace Book Award from the Friends of the Minnesota Valley Regional Library. Finally, the heartwarming story of a boy and his dogs won the Michigan Young Readers Award, Division II, from the Michigan Council of Teachers of English.

Many people have praised the book and Wilson Rawls. An Amazon.com critic said: "This unforgettable classic belongs on every child's bookshelf." An AudioFile critic was just as impressed with the book. "In spite of being written during the Depression, there is a timelessness to this simple story," the critic wrote. "Rawls instills this autobiographical piece with a strong sense of right and wrong, as well as innocence and integrity. This title is an excellent selection for anyone desiring an uplifting, but realistic tale." Another critic called *Where the Red Fern Grows* "an exciting tale of love and adventure you'll never forget."

Young critics like the book just as much as grown-up critics. One young reader wrote: "*Where the Red Fern Grows* was truly a story of a young boy and his dogs, and the special relationship that grew between them. I really enjoyed reading this book, and I would recommend it highly to any boy or girl who likes to read stories about people and their pets. If you read this story, you'll realize that dogs really are man's best friends!"

A teenage reader thought *Where the Red Fern Grows* was the best book she had ever read:

> It is so superb that I would rate it six stars if I could. If I only were allowed to read one book in my whole life, this would be the book definitely. . . . Although the ending is not a happy one and will leave everyone in tears, this twist of plot adds to the flawlessness of this amazing story. Everyone absolutely must read this book, regardless of age. I read this book when I was fifteen, and I did not find it too childish or simple, and I believe I will reread it again some day, because I believe that every read will bring different feelings and memories to me.

Where the Red Fern Grows became so popular that in 1972 a film agent from Hollywood came to visit Wilson Rawls at his home in Idaho Falls, Idaho. The agent wanted to make the book into a movie! When the agent agreed not to change the book's title, the characters' names, or the story itself, Rawls agreed. The agent left. Two years passed. Since they did not hear from Hollywood, Rawls and his wife decided that the book was not going to be made into a movie after all.

One summer day in 1974, Wilson Rawls and his wife were getting ready to go fishing, one of their favorite activities. As they were walking out the door, the telephone rang. It was the agent calling from Oklahoma. He wanted them to drive to Rawls's childhood home in Oklahoma. "Not having anything better to do at the time, we decided to go," he said.

"When we arrived I'd never seen such excitement," Rawls said. "The road to the river was blocked for a mile or so with cars and people. We finally made our way to the gate where a guard was posted. Still not knowing what to expect, I told the guard I was Rawls and I thought someone was expecting us. 'They sure are,' the guard said, and told us to walk down to the river."

What do you think they discovered by the river? Rawls's old home was there, completely rebuilt! The movie company had hired Cherokee Indians to build a copy of the Rawlses' house and farm. It was the movie set. The movie of *Where the Red Fern Grows* was being filmed after all! The famous actor James Whitmore played the role of Grandpa. Beverly Garland played Mama, and Jack Ging was Papa. Stewart Peterson, a new actor, got the lead role as Billy. Wilson Rawls got a part, too—he was the narrator! Many people enjoyed seeing the movie after they had read the book.

When the filming was completed, the house was moved to an Indian village. Tourists can visit it and see how Rawls and his family lived in the 1930s. Because of his Cherokee heritage (remember his mother was part Cherokee Indian), this meant a lot to Rawls.

Thinking about what others think of
Where the Red Fern Grows

- Do you think the book would have been better with a happy ending? Why or why not?
- One critic said that Wilson Rawls is "a straightforward, shoot-from-the-hip storyteller with a searingly honest voice." What parts of this book did you find honest? in what ways?
- Imagine that you are choosing actors to portray the main characters for a new movie of *Where the Red Fern Grows.* Whom would you choose to play Billy, his parents, and Grandpa? What makes these actors right for these roles?

Glossary

Here are some important words and terms from *Where the Red Fern Grows*. Understanding these words will make it easier for you to read and appreciate the novel.

bawling crying loudly like a baby

blizzard a powerful, dangerous snowstorm

breed a particular type of dog. Beagles, poodles, and huskies are different breeds of dogs.

clothesline Clean wet clothes are hung on a line of rope to dry. The clothesline is hung outside in good weather and inside in bad weather.

coon short for "raccoon"

crawfish a type of shellfish that looks like a small lobster (also spelled "crayfish")

Depression the Great Depression, the economic crisis that began with the stock market crash in 1929 and continued through the 1930s

dumbfounded speechless with shock and amazement

fern a leafy green plant, often tall and feathery-looking

gratitude a feeling of being grateful and thankful

grieve to feel very sad, usually because a loved one has died

hounds hunting dogs

minnows small freshwater fish used for bait

pangs sudden, brief pains or emotions

pelts animal skins with the hair or fur still attached, usually from animals such as raccoons, beavers, and bears

ringtail nickname for a raccoon. Raccoons are often called ringtails because their tails have rings of darker fur.

romp to play in a noisy, carefree, and energetic way

rural country

sacred holy

sacrifice to give up something important and enjoyable for a good reason

sycamore a type of tree

switch a bundle of twigs. In the novel, Billy's parents hit him with a switch when he misbehaves.

trail a path, usually in the woods

tree to chase up a tree

unbearable intolerable, too painful or unpleasant to cope with

"Son, a man can do anything he sets
out to do, if he doesn't give up."

—Wilson Rawls's father

Wilson Rawls never forgot his father's words. These words gave him the courage to try to become a writer.

After he published *Where the Red Fern Grows*, Wilson Rawls wrote just one more book. It is called *Summer of the Monkeys* and you'll like it, too. Even when he was a big success, Wilson Rawls never forgot the hard time he had learning to write and getting his book published. He wanted to make it easier for children to achieve their goals, especially the goal of becoming a writer.

To help kids get the courage to reach for *their* dreams, Rawls visited many schools around the country. He visited more than twenty-two states! Rawls told students how he decided to become a writer when he read Jack London's *Call of the Wild.* He explained how the book was his first real treasure. Wilson Rawls dreamed big, but he never dreamed that someday there would be thousands of children who would carry around *his* book as a treasure.

He told the children how hard it was for him to make his dream come true because he only went to school for a short time. He did not know how to spell. He did not know much grammar, either. He told the children that when he was a child, he was too poor to buy paper and pencils.

Rawls always took along the manuscript of *Where the Red Fern Grows* to show the children. A manuscript is a rough draft of a book before it has been edited, revised, and proofread. The manuscript Wilson Rawls showed to the children had a lot of writing mistakes. Why did he show the rough draft? "I want to stress to them," he explained, "how important it is to learn to spell, punctuate, and mainly how important it is for them to stay in school."

Rawls's letter to the world

So many people asked Wilson Rawls for advice about becoming a successful writer that he decided to put his advice in writing. Here is his letter:

For Those Who Want to Be Writers:

Even though I can't tell you how to be a writer, maybe I can give you some pointers.

Do a lot of reading. Study the style of authors you admire but do not try to copy their style. You will have to find a style of your own. Write in a way that is natural for you.

Read all the books you can find on creative writing. Your librarian can help you find books that will help you.

Do not wait to start writing. You are never too young to start. Your first story should be based on something you know well. Make it exciting. Do not worry about grammar and punctuation on your first draft. The important thing is to get the story down on paper. It will probably need a lot of revising and rewriting. You can worry about grammar and punctuation then. Remember, the more you write, the better you will be.

Don't get discouraged. If you can keep on trying and don't give up, you will make it someday. The road can be rough but the day you see your work in print makes it all worth it.

Best of luck!

Sincerely,
Wilson Rawls

Attention, all writers!

Rawls's struggle to become a writer shows the importance of not giving up. His hard work and determination prove the importance of the old saying, "If at first you don't succeed, try, try again."

- **Books that change a life**: Wilson Rawls decided to become a writer after he read *The Call of the Wild* by Jack London. Read *The Call of the Wild*, and write a little about the story. Then, explain why you think this book made Wilson Rawls want to be a writer. What parts of the book do you think he liked the best? Why?

You can also choose a book that changed *your* life. It might be a make-believe story, such as a novel or possibly the real-life story of a person, such as a biography or an autobiography. First, summarize the story. Then, explain how the book changed your life. What parts had the strongest influence on your life? Give specific reasons explaining why the book is important to you.

- **My life and welcome to it!:** *Where the Red Fern Grows* is the real-life story of Wilson Rawls's life growing up on a small farm in the Ozarks. The story takes place from the time Wilson/Billy is ten years old to the time he is around twelve years old. Choose two years in your life that have been very important to you. Perhaps the two years take place when you were five to seven years old, when you first started school. They might be when you were eight to ten, when your family moved or you got a new baby brother or sister. Tell the story of your life in the first-person point of view, as Wilson Rawls did. Show all the events through your eyes. Use the pronouns "I" and "me." Add lots of details to make your story interesting, just as Wilson Rawls did.

- **Write a legend:** Billy is very sad when his dogs die. However, he feels better when he sees the red fern on their grave because of the Indian legend of the red fern. He is sure the red fern has come from an angel. He thinks this means his dogs are in heaven. A legend is a story handed down through time that explains how or why something in nature originated. Legends are sometimes based on facts from nature or history. Often, however, they have wild details and characters. Write a legend to explain what has happened to Billy's dogs after they die. Make the legend happy so it gives Billy some comfort.

- **Debate whether people should hunt:** In the Ozarks in the 1930s, hunting was a way of life. People hunted for food and for animal pelts. They ate the meat and sold the pelts to earn money. To Billy and his neighbors, hunting is also a sport. The big championship hunt shows this.

Even today, many people hunt. Some animals such as deer and rabbits are hunted for both sport and food. Other animals, such as tigers and lions, are hunted just for sport. However, not everyone feels that people should hunt animals for food or sport.

Write a make-believe dialogue between Billy and someone who doesn't understand hunting. You could also write the dialogue between Billy and someone who doesn't think people should hunt, even for food. Be sure to use quotation marks to show each character's dialogue.

Activities

- **Learn about our best friend:** Billy loves his dogs, Little Ann and Old Dan. Billy is not the only person who loves his dogs. There are nearly 58 million pet dogs in America alone! But Billy's dogs, like many dogs around the world, are far more than pets: They are helpers.

Ever since dogs and humans got together, dogs have been trained to help people. Billy's hounds, Old Dan and Little Ann, hunt for food and valuable pelts. The Seeing Eye Foundation trains guide dogs to help people with impaired vision become more independent. Canine Companions for Independence trains dogs to help disabled people, such as those who have cerebral palsy. In wartime, dogs have served as messengers, guards, and rescue dogs. In peacetime, dogs search for people who are buried in snow or trapped in rubble from fires.

Choose one way that dogs help people. Do some research to learn more about the way they help. You can look on the Internet, in magazines, or interview people who train or use dogs in their jobs and lives. Share your findings in an oral report or on a Web page. You might also want to invite a person from the Seeing Eye Foundation, Canine Companions for Independence, or the police department to demonstrate how they train and use dogs as helpers.

• **Go on an ecology hunt:** Ecology (ee-**kol**-uh-jee) is the study of plants, animals, and their environment. Billy knows a lot about ecology because he spends most of his time in the woods. Learn about the ecology of your area by going on an ecology hunt. Take a look-and-see hunt by finding the things on the list below. Look and see, but don't touch!

First, copy the list into a notebook. Then, go outside with a buddy or small group of friends and look around. When you find an item, check it off on your list. Last, draw a simple picture of it. (You may find it helpful to bring along a nature guidebook, which will help you identify specific plants and animals. Visit your school or public library to get some suggestions from a librarian.) Remember: You're visiting living things, so don't disturb their home. Be careful not to touch any of the plants or animals.

acorn or other large tree seed	moss
animal footprint	mushroom
ant	rock with many colors
beetle	sand
bird	small seed
butterfly	spiderweb
caterpillar	squirrel
feather	tree
fern	twig
flower	worm
leaf	

• **Play a game from Billy's childhood:** Billy and his sisters don't have a lot of time to play games. When they do have fun, they don't play video games, ride skateboards, or go bowling like you might do! Billy and his sisters play games like hopscotch and jacks. Play a game of jacks to get a taste of life in the 1930s. Jacks is played with two people. Here's how to do it.

You will need a small ball that fits into the palm of your hand and ten small objects. They can be shells, pebbles, beans, or jacks (metal or plastic X shapes). The object of the game is to pick up the jacks on one bounce of the ball. You have to catch the ball before it hits the ground a second time. Follow these three easy steps to play.

1. Sit on the ground. Put all ten jacks in your hand. Then, toss them on the ground. They must stay where they land. You cannot move them.

2. Toss the ball in the air. Pick up one jack—but don't touch any other jacks! Keep the jack in your hand, and catch the ball after it bounces on the ground once.

3. If you miss the ball, touch any other jack, or drop your jack, you lose your turn.

Keep playing until one player picks up all ten jacks, one by one. For the next round, toss all the jacks again and now pick them up two jacks at a time. Then, play by picking up three jacks at a time, four jacks at a time, and so on.

• **Map it!:** At the end of the novel, the grown-up Billy says: "I have never been back to the Ozarks. All I have left are my dreams and memories, but if God is willing, some day I'd like to go back—back to those beautiful hills. . . . Once again I'd like to face a mountain breeze and smell the wonderful scent of the redbuds, and pawpaws, and the dogwoods. With my hands I'd like to caress the cool white bark of a sycamore." Billy loves the Ozarks. That's no surprise because the Ozarks are a beautiful area!

The Ozarks cover a large area in the south-central part of the United States. The Ozarks include parts of four states: Arkansas, Kansas, Missouri, and Oklahoma. Make a map showing the Ozark region. Use markers, crayons, or different-colored clay to show the mountains, valleys, and rivers in the area. Be sure to show the borders for each of the four states. Label major cities, mountains, and rivers.

• **Make a miniworld:** A terrarium is a small, closed world. It is made up of plants, soil, water, and air. In some ways, Billy's childhood home is like a terrarium because it is closed off from the rest of the world. Very few people visited the backwoods of Oklahoma during the 1930s.

Make your own terrarium and learn how to keep the earth healthy, as Billy and his family does. You will need the following things:

- a clear plastic or glass jar with a wide mouth, such as an applesauce or peanut butter jar
- 2 handfuls of pebbles or sand
- 2 handfuls of soil
- 1 handful of dead leaves
- 1 handful of moss
- several small plants, such as ferns or flowers
- a long stick
- water

Now, follow these steps to create your miniworld:

1. Wash and dry the jar. Remove any labels.

2. Put the sand in the bottom of the jar. Then, put in the soil. Next, put in the dead leaves.

3. Using the stick, make holes in the soil and add your plants. Place the moss around the plants.

4. Sprinkle a *little* water on the plants.

5. Cover the jar with the lid. Place your miniworld in the light, but not in direct sunlight. See how your miniworld changes over the weeks and months.

• **Meet Rocky Raccoon:** Billy describes the raccoons' sneaky tricks. Raccoons have many ways to outsmart hunters! Billy and Grandpa talk about how curious raccoons are and how much they love shiny objects. Grandpa says, "You see, a coon is a curious little animal. Anything that is bright and shiny attracts him. He will reach in and pull it out."

Find out more about these interesting wild creatures. How many species or kinds of raccoons are there? What do they look like? How big are they? Where do they live? What do they eat? How do they raise their young? Do they make good house pets? Why or why not? Make a poster to share your findings.

• **Cook up some corn bread!:** Billy's family eats a lot of corn bread. That's because corn bread is good—and good for you. The first settlers learned from the Indians the good things you can do with corn. Here is an easy and fun recipe for corn bread just like

Billy and his family ate. Because you will be using the oven, make some corn bread with a parent, an older brother or sister, or an older friend.

Ingredients

1 cup yellow cornmeal

1 cup flour

2 tablespoons sugar

4 teaspoons baking powder (not baking *soda!*)

½ teaspoon salt

1 cup milk

¼ cup butter or margarine

1 egg

Directions

1. Preheat oven to 425° Fahrenheit.

2. Wash your hands.

3. Rub some butter or margarine in a square pan. You can use a pan 8 inches wide and 2 inches high or one that is 9 inches wide and 2 inches high.

4. In a big bowl, mix all the ingredients. Mix until blended, no more than one to two minutes.

5. Pour the batter into the pan.

6. Bake 20–25 minutes until golden brown.

Variation: You can make corn muffins by baking the batter in muffin cups. This batter will fill 12 cups. Bake about 15 minutes.

Related Reading

Other book by Wilson Rawls
Summer of the Monkeys (1976)

Dog books—fiction
Call of the Wild by Jack London
Danger Dog by Lynn Hal
A Dog Called Kitty by Bill Wallace
Foxy by Helen Griffith
Kävik, the Wolf Dog by Walt Morey
Lassie Come-Home by Eric Knight
Old Yeller Fred Gipson
Rascal by Sterling North
Savage Sam by Fred Gipson
Saving Shiloh by Phyllis Reynolds Naylor
Shiloh by Phyllis Reynolds Naylor
Shiloh Season by Phyllis Reynolds Naylor
Sounder by William Howard Armstrong
Stone Fox by John Reynolds Gardiner
White Fang by Jack London
The Wolfling by Sterling North

Dog books—nonfiction
All About Dogs and Puppies by Laura Driscoll
Puppy: Pet Care Guide for Kids by Mark Evans

The Complete Dog Book for Kids by the American Kennel Club
Dog by Juliet Clutton-Brock
Dog Training for Kids by Carol Lea Benjamin
Dog Tricks by Arthur J. Haggerty
Puppy Training for Kids by Sarah Whitehead
Totally Fun Things to Do with Your Dog by Maxine Rock
Understanding Man's Best Friend: Why Dogs Look and Act the Way They Do by Ann Squire

Books about raccoons
Raccoon on His Own by Jim Arnosky
Raccoons and Ripe Corn by Jim Arnosky
Welcome to the World of Raccoons by Diane Swanson

Books about hunting
Field Trips: Bug Hunting, Animal Tracking, Bird-Watching, Shore Walking with Jim Arnosky by Jim Arnosky
Tracks and Trailcraft: A Fully Illustrated Guide for the Identification of Animal Tracks in Forest and Field, Barnyard and Backyard by Ellsworth Jaeger

Audiocassettes
Where the Red Fern Grows is available as a three-cassette audio, read by actor Richard Thomas (Bantam) or by Frank Muller (Recorded Books).

Movies
Where the Red Fern Grows (1974)
Where the Red Fern Grows II (1992)

Books

Children's Literature Review. Volume 9. Detroit: The Gale Group, Inc., 1985.

Contemporary Literary Criticism. Volume 21. Detroit: The Gale Group, Inc., 1982.

Dictionary of Literary Biography, Volume 52: *American Writers for Children Since 1960*: Fiction. Detroit: The Gale Group, Inc., 1986.

Kovacs, Deborah and James Preller. *Meet the Authors and Illustrators.* New York: Scholastic Inc, 1991.

Rees, David. *The Marble on the Water: Essays on Contemporary Writers of Fiction for Children and Young Adults.* Boston: Horn Book, 1980.

Something About the Author Autobiography Series. Volume 5. Detroit: The Gale Group, Inc., 1988.

Newspapers and magazines

Booklist, August 1995, Volume 91, Number 22, p. 1966.

Booklist, March 15, 1996, Volume 92, Number 14, p. 1306.

The Horn Book Magazine, January–February 1996, Volume 72, Number 1, p. 105.

Knight Ridder/Tribune News Service, April 15, 1999, p. K0987.

Reading Today, December 2001, Volume 19, p. 41.

Saturday Evening Post, April 1986, Volume 258, p. 68.

Saturday Evening Post, March 1986, Volume 248, p. 50.

Web sites

Contemporary Authors Online, The Gale Group, Inc., 2002.
Reproduced in Biography Resource. Farmington Hills, Mich.:
The Gale Group, 2002.
www.galenet.com/servlet/BioRC

Idaho Falls Public Library:
pac.eils.lib.id.us/rawls.html

Educational Paperback Association:
www.edupaperback.org/authorbios/Rawls_Wilson.html

Houghton Mifflin Education Place:
www.eduplace.com/kids/hmr/mtai/rawls.html

Random House Children's Books:
www.randomhouse.com/teachers/authors/rawls.html

Trelease-on-Reading:
www.trelease-on-reading.com/rawls.html